AROUND ONE CACTUS

Owls, Bats and Leaping Rats

By Anthony D. Fredericks

Illustrated by Jennifer DiRubbio

Dedication:
To Julie Valin for her warm friendship, constant support, and infectious humor...may they always be celebrated! — ADF

To my parents: Mom for cultivating a childhood dream, and Dad for your interest in wildlife which inspired my love of nature. — JDR

Copyright © 2003 Anthony D. Fredericks
Illustrations copyright © 2003 Jennifer DiRubbio Lubinsky
A Sharing Nature With Children Book

Library of Congress Cataloging-in-Publication Data

Fredericks, Anthony D.
   Around one cactus : owls, bats, and leaping rats / by Anthony D. Fredericks ; illustrated by Jennifer DiRubbio.— 1st ed.
       p. cm. — (A sharing nature with children book)
Summary: A child sees a saguaro cactus by day but there are no animals until after he leaves, when various creatures come out to play and prey. Also includes "field notes" which provide more facts about desert animals.
   ISBN 1-58469-051-8 (hardcover) — ISBN 1-58469-052-6 (pbk.)
   1. Desert animals—Juvenile literature. [1. Desert animals.] I. DiRubbio, Jennifer, ill. II. Title. III. Series.
   QL116.F74 2003
   591.754—dc21

                                   2003003660

Dawn Publications
12402 Bitney Springs Road
Nevada City, CA 95959
800-545-7475
nature@dawnpub.com

Printed in Korea

10 9 8 7 6 5 4 3 2 1
First Edition
Design and computer production by Andrea Miles

Dear Two-Legged Adventurer,

Welcome to my hot and rocky home! You may think that this place is lifeless and dull, but it's not. In fact, the more you learn about the desert the more amazing it becomes. I think the desert is a topic you can really sink your teeth into. Get it?

The desert is filled with amazing creatures and incredible plants. Some of us are friends, some of us aren't. But that's OK, because we have all learned to adapt to our special environment. That means that we can survive and reproduce. It also means that there are many kinds of neighbors who like to live in the same place. Some neighbors may be dangerous, like me. And some, like the bat, may spend the whole night sticking its face into flowers. We're all special.

Many of us live in and around the saguaro cactus—it's really a sharp place to be! Some live high above in lofty apartments. Others hide between rocks on the ground. And a few live underground where it's cool.

I hope you enjoy visiting our unique home. We're an unusual band of neighbors—some fly, some slither, some hop and a few even dance in the moonlight. Look around, but be careful where you walk!

Warm regards,

W.D.

(Western Diamondback Rattlesnake)

This is the desert, wild and free,
  A place of sun-baked majesty,
With shifting dunes and rocky edges
  And bushes gripping ancient ledges.
Here stands a cactus, tall and grand,
  A haven for creatures in a waterless land.

This is the cactus.

The prickly cactus with arms raised high
  Was watched by a boy with a curious eye.
"Who could be living on this arid ground?"
  He asked as the breeze tumbled all around.

He observed the giant in the fading light,
But the critters were resting far from sight.
So he turned and slowly walked away.
Then the creatures woke to play and prey.

A leaping **rat** builds a cozy nest
   (A sheltered place for her young to rest)
Beside the cactus tall and grand,
   A haven for creatures in a waterless land.

A tiny **owl** with perfect sight,
  Who sleeps by day and hunts by night,
Lives high above her neighbor's nest
  (A special place for young to rest)
Beside the cactus tall and grand,
  A haven for creatures in a waterless land.

A long-nose **bat** flies to this tower
  And spreads the pollen from flower to flower,
Above the owl with perfect sight,
  Who sleeps by day and hunts by night,
Who lives above her neighbor's nest
  (A special place for young to rest)
Beside the cactus tall and grand,
  A haven for creatures in a waterless land.

A **rattlesnake** with deadly teeth
  Slips-slides across the ground beneath
The long-nose bat upon the tower,
  Who spreads the pollen from flower to flower,
Above the owl with perfect sight,
  Who sleeps by day and hunts by night,
Who lives above her neighbor's nest
  (A special place for young to rest)
Beside the cactus tall and grand,
  A haven for creatures in a waterless land.

Some **scorpions** with stinging tails
  Dance along on unseen trails,
Past rattlesnakes with deadly teeth
  Slip-sliding on the ground beneath
The long-nose bat upon the tower,
  Who spreads the pollen from flower to flower,
Above the owl with perfect sight,
  Who sleeps by day and hunts by night,
Who lives above her neighbor's nest
  (A special place for young to rest)
Beside the cactus tall and grand,
  A haven for creatures in a waterless land.

A den of **foxes** starts to stir.
  They clean and groom their light brown fur,
While eyeing scorpions with stinging tails
  Who dance along on unseen trails,
Past rattlesnakes with deadly teeth
  Slip-sliding on the ground beneath
The long-nose bat upon the tower,
  Who spreads the pollen from flower to flower,
Above the owl with perfect sight,
  Who sleeps by day and hunts by night,
Who lives above her neighbor's nest
  (A special place for young to rest)
Beside the cactus tall and grand,
  A haven for creatures in a waterless land.

A **gila monster** with painted back
  Crawls from a hole in search of a snack,
Near foxes who begin to stir
  And clean and groom their light brown fur,
While eyeing scorpions with stinging tails
  Who dance along on unseen trails,
Past rattlesnakes with deadly teeth
  Slip-sliding on the ground beneath
The long-nose bat upon the tower,
  Who spreads the pollen from flower to flower,
Above the owl with perfect sight,
  Who sleeps by day and hunts by night,
Who lives above her neighbor's nest
  (A special place for young to rest)
Beside the cactus tall and grand,
  A haven for creatures in a waterless land.

A world of survivors in a sun-baked land
Are sheltered and harbored by a cactus grand.
The spiny plant with its weathered face
Is a noble guard in this busy place.

Field Notes

All of the animals described in this book are found in the Sonoran desert of the southwestern United States and northern Mexico. The specific species illustrated are all nocturnal: they sleep during the day and come out in the cool of night to hunt and feed. These creatures can all be found in or around a Saguaro cactus.

Saguaro Cactus

The Saguaro (suh-WAR-oh) Cactus lives exclusively in the Sonoran desert. The Saguaro provides food, shelter and moisture for a wide variety of desert animals. It thrives in rocky areas from sea level to 4,500 feet in elevation. It requires very little water and can go for two years without rain. It has a root system that is shallow and wide-reaching. This allows for quick absorption of water when it rains. Surprisingly, about 75 to 95 percent of the cactus's weight is water. The saguaro doesn't begin to grow "arms" until it is at least 70 years old. From May to June many large, white, waxy flowers blossom on the Saguaro. The Saguaro flower is the Arizona state flower.

Fantastic Fact: Saguaros can grow as tall as 56 feet, weigh as much as an African elephant, and live to be over 200 years old.

Kangaroo Rat

This animal's name comes from the fact that it hops over the ground in much the same way as a kangaroo. There are twenty-two different species of kangaroo rats in North America. They are found only in the more arid regions of the western and southwestern United States. Kangaroo rats reach an overall length of nine to 14 inches (including the tail) and are often pale in color with shades of tan, cream and off-white. Their hind feet are large with hairy soles that aid in jumping in loose, soft sand. They live in underground burrows shaped like the letter U. They primarily eat seeds which they gather from various plants at night. Their life span is less than five years.

Fantastic Fact: All animals generate water when digesting carbohydrates. Kangaroo rats, however, are so efficient at converting the dry seeds they eat into water that they need no other water source. They do not sweat or pant to keep cool as other animals do.

Elf Owl

Elf owls live in the abandoned nests of gila woodpeckers. Typically, their nests are 15 to 35 feet above the ground. Babies stay in the nest until they are about one month old. Because of the moisture stored in the cactus and the thick lining of the nest, an elf owl stays cool even when the air temperature is over 100 degrees. Elf owls are tiny birds with rounded heads, yellow eyes, a greenish-yellow bill and white eyebrows. They eat insects, spiders, and other small animals such as lizards and centipedes. They can be easily identified by their high-pitched squeaky whistle.

Fantastic Fact: The elf owl is the world's smallest owl. Adults grow to a length of just five inches and a total weight of one and a half ounces.

Lesser Long-Nose Bat

This creature rests in caves during the day and feeds at night. Its eyes are best adapted for seeing in the dark, although it only sees in black and white. It plays a critical role in the life of the saguaro. When the saguaro blossoms in May, buds emerge at the tops of its long arms. These buds open up into large white flowers with yellow centers. Each flower opens only once, and it does so in the cool of the night. The long-nose bat swoops in and sips the nectar inside the flowers. As it drinks, pollen sticks to the bat's face and is carried to the next flower. This is one way the saguaro cactus is pollinated. White-winged doves are the primary pollinators of saguaro flowers.

Fantastic Fact: The smallest bat, the Bumblebee Bat, has a body length of one inch and a wingspan of six inches. The largest bat in the world, the Flying Fox, has a body length of one foot and a wingspan of more than six feet.

Rattlesnake

Rattlesnakes belong to a group of poisonous snakes known as pit vipers. These snakes have small depressions, or pits, on both sides of their faces. These pits are used as temperature detectors to help them locate prey in the dark. The rattle at the end of a rattlesnake's tail is made of dry, horny rings of skin that interlock with each other. They never shake the rattle when hunting—that would spoil the hunt. When they shake it they are announcing their presence, warning that they are dangerous, and asking to be left alone. The rattlesnake's venom, or poison, is produced in a large gland behind the eyes. When a rattlesnake bites, its fangs enter and leave the victim in less than a second. The poison is injected into the victim through both fangs. There are ten species of rattlesnakes in Arizona. Their diet may include small warm-blooded animals such as rodents and rabbits, birds, and lizards.

Fantastic Fact: A rattlesnake's fangs are "folded" back into its mouth when not in use. Just as amazing, rattlers essentially have two pairs of eyes. The pits in front of their eyes form infrared images that sense the smallest of temperature changes; in short, they supplement the normal eyes' vision.

Scorpions

There are more than 1,300 species of scorpions worldwide. Although some species have as many as twelve eyes, scorpions have very poor eyesight. They have sense organs on their bellies to detect chemical trails of their own species. In addition, they rely on their sense of touch to locate prey. Often, a scorpion walks around with its claws spread apart until it bumps into a tasty spider or insect. Only then does it capture its victim! Sometimes it may use its powerful stinger. A scorpion's stinger is a hollow tube connected to a poison gland near the end of its tail. During mating season, males and females will grasp claws and dance around in circles. Interestingly, scorpions are related to crabs and lobsters.

Fantastic Fact: The smallest scorpion in the world is only two tenths of an inch long. The largest scorpion, the South African Scorpion, is over eight inches long.

Kit Fox

Kit foxes live throughout the desert regions of North America. Adults have a slender body, narrow skull, long nose and a long bushy tail. Their pale color makes them nearly invisible against light-colored desert sands. The soles of their feet are hairy, which helps them walk on loose sand. They also have large ears that stand up straight in the air. When the desert breeze blows over them, it cools the blood inside. Then the blood circulates, cooling the rest of the body. After mating, about four to five babies are born, usually between February and April. During the first month of life they are nursed by the mother while the father hunts for food. Kit fox families stay together until the young are ready to live on their own. They feed on rodents, squirrels, rabbits, insects and birds. When running, they can reach speeds of up to 25 miles per hour.

Fantastic Fact: A baby kit fox needs to eat about 100 pounds of meat during its first two months of life. That's about 800 kangaroo rats.

Gila Monster

The Gila monster, named for the Gila River Basin in Arizona, is a descendent of some of the oldest animals on earth. Its relatives go back nearly 50 million years. A Gila monster has black, orange, pink or yellows splotches and spots on its body. It also has small bead-like scales across its back. This lizard's diet consists of eggs, lizards, birds and mice. Gila monsters prefer to eat their prey whole, often swallowing them in one or two gulps. An adult Gila monster grows to 18 inches in length. It prefers to live in rocky desert areas hiding among rock ledges. It has a poisonous bite; however they are not aggressive toward humans.

Fantastic Fact: The Gila monster and the Mexican Beaded Lizard are the only two poisonous lizards in the world.

How to Learn More

Dear Reader,

Ecology is the study of animals and their environment. Here are some of my favorite resources about desert ecology:

Saguaro Moon: A Desert Journal (2002) by Kristin Joy Pratt-Serafini, a wonderful way to learn about the desert through the journal of a long-time nature lover.

Desert Song (2000) by Tony Johnson, a book that takes a look at the amazing desert creatures that come out at night to hunt and play.

Cactus Hotel (1991) by Brenda Z. Guiberson, the growth and long life of a saguaro cactus is vividly detailed in this wondrous book.

Desert Giant: The World of the Saguaro Cactus (1989) by Barbara Bash, easy-to-read text and colorful illustrations document the life cycle of this amazing cactus tree.

Cactus Poems (1998) by Frank Asch, is a collection of engaging poetry about the cactus as well as other life forms that inhabit this special ecosystem.

America's Deserts (1996) by Marianne D. Wallace, vividly portrays the flora and fauna of the four desert regions in North America.

One Small Square: Cactus Desert (1995) by Donald Silver, presents a dazzling cast of creatures interacting with each other and the amazing plants that inhabit this very special place.

A Saguaro Cactus (1999) by Jen Green, offers an intriguing look into the incredible variety of creatures and critters that live in and around a Saguaro cactus.

Here are some of the other children's books I've written.

Animal Sharpshooters (1999), an examination of animals that throw things at other animals.

Elephants for Kids (1999), the story about elephants and their lives as told through the eyes of a 10-year-old boy.

In One Tidepool (2002), a poetic journey to a wild and splashy place filled with colorful and amazing animals.

Slugs (2001), amazing information and eye-popping photographs about a greatly misunderstood creature.

Tsunami Man: Learning About Killer Waves with Walter Dudley (2002), a look at one of nature's most misunderstood natural disasters.

Under One Rock (2001), a rhythmic description of the colorful creatures that live together beneath a single rock.

Weird Walkers (2000), a book about a lizard that walks on water, a fish that walks on land, and an animal that walks upside down.

Here are the names and addresses of organizations working hard to preserve animal habitats. You might want to contact them to find out what they are doing and how you can become involved.

Arizona-Sonora Desert Museum
2021 N. Kinney Road
Tucson, AZ 85743
520-883-1380 • www.desertmuseum.org

National Wildlife Federation
11100 Wildlife Center Drive
Reston, VA 20190
800-822-9919 • www.nwf.org

National Audubon Society
700 Broadway
New York, NY 10003
212-979-3000 • www.audubon.org

Nature Conservancy
1815 North Lynn Street
Arlington, VA 22209
800-628-6860 • www.nature.org

If you or your teacher would like to learn more about me and the books I write, please log on to my web site, www.afredericks.com

Anthony D. Fredericks is a veteran nature explorer. He grew up on the beaches of southern California and during summers hiked the Sierra Nevada mountains of eastern California. Later he attended high school in the high desert region of Arizona where his love of desert life blossomed. While a student at the University of Arizona in Tucson he often spent his free time trekking through and exploring the Sonoran desert. Now Tony explores the mountainside in Pennsylvania where he and his wife live. A former classroom teacher and reading specialist, he is Professor of Education at York College. As the author of more than 25 children's books he is a frequent visitor to schools around the country, where he shares the wonders of nature with a new generation of naturalists.

Jennifer DiRubbio is both a passionate artist and an avid environmentalist. She has been active as an artist for several organizations that promote nature and a healthy planet. Jennifer graduated with a BFA from Pratt Institute in 1992. She keeps her home and studio in Merrick, New York, as "green" and environmentally sound as possible, where her husband and young child also work and play.

ALSO BY ANTHONY FREDERICKS AND JENNIFER DIRUBBIO

Under One Rock: Bugs, Slugs and Other Ughs. A whole community of creatures lives under rocks. No child will be able to resist taking a peek after reading this.

In One Tidepool: Crabs, Snails and Salty Tails. Have you ever ventured to the edge of the sea and peered into a tidepool? A colorful community of creatures lives there!

A FEW OTHER NATURE AWARENESS BOOKS FROM DAWN PUBLICATIONS

This is the Sea that Feeds Us, by Robert F. Baldwin. In simple cumulative verse, this book explores the oceans' fabulous food web that reaches all the way from plankton to people.

Birds in Your Backyard by Barbara Herkert, can help kindle the spark of interest in birds at an early age, portraying common backyard species found all over the North America.

Do Animals Have Feelings, Too? by David Rice presents fascinating true stories of animal behavior, and asks the reader whether they think the animals' actions show feelings or instinct.

A Tree in the Ancient Forest, by Carol Reed-Jones. The plants and animals around and under a grand old fir are remarkably connected to each other.

Stickeen: John Muir and the Brave Little Dog, by Donnell Rubay, is a true wilderness adventure that transformed the relationship between Muir and a dog.

Motherlove, by Virginia Kroll. Animals of many kinds show the qualities of motherhood as they feed, guide, protect, instruct, comfort, and love their young.

Two books by Joseph Anthony, *The Dandelion Seed* and *In A Nutshell* are both stories—the travels of a wind-blown dandelion seed and the life cycle of an acorn—and metaphors for life.

Three books by J. Patrick Lewis, *Earth & You—A Closer View; Earth & Us—Continuous;* and *Earth & Me—Our Family Tree,* introduce the major habitats, the continuity of life and the connections between animals and their environment.

Dawn Publications is dedicated to inspiring in children a deeper understanding and appreciation for all life on Earth. To order, or for a copy of our catalog, please call 800-545-7475. Please also visit our web site at www.dawnpub.com.